ULTIMATE
4 Ingredient
RECIPIES

Meals in Minutes

by Sheryn R. Jones
A Cookbook Resources book

Mud Puddle inc.
NEW YORK

Ultimate 4 Ingredient Recipes
Meals in Minutes
By Sheryn R. Jones

Portions of the book were previously published

Copyright © 2012 by Cookbook Resources, LLC,
A Mud Puddle, Inc. company

Mud Puddle, Inc.
36 W. 25th Street
New York, NY 10010
info@mudpuddleinc.com

ISBN: 978-1-59769-091-1

Title page art by Natalya Levish, used under
license from Shutterstock.com.

Oreo is a registered trademark of Nabisco
(Mondelēz International).

2 4 6 8 10 9 7 5 3 1
Printed in China December 2016

Table of Contents

Introduction

In our fast-paced, rush-here-and-there lives, a home-cooked meal may be considered a luxury. We live out of our cars, placing food orders on cell phones and going to drive-through windows for the night's meal—and maybe the family sits down together to eat.

We want to help families come back to the table and spend quality time together while sharing good food. The recipes in *Ultimate 4 Ingredient Cookbook* are easy to prepare and the ingredients are readily available. Most of them are already in your pantry.

Everyone in the family can cook out of *Ultimate 4 Ingredient Cookbook*. Mouth-watering meals are just minutes away and every minute we spend around the table enriches our lives and helps us grow stronger.

Please enjoy and don't hesitate to recruit some helpers!

Appetizers

Artichoke-Bacon Dip

1 (14 ounce) jar marinated
 artichoke hearts, drained,
 chopped
1 cup mayonnaise

2 teaspoons Worcestershire
 sauce
5 slices bacon, cooked crisp,
 crumbled

- Preheat oven to 350°.
- Combine all ingredients in large bowl. Pour into sprayed 8-inch baking dish.
- Bake for 12 minutes. Yields 1½ cups.

Chippy Beef Dip

1 (8 ounce) package cream
 cheese, softened
1 (8 ounce) carton sour cream

1 (2.5 ounce) jar sliced dried beef,
 cubed
½ cup finely chopped pecans

- Beat cream cheese and sour cream in bowl until creamy.
- Fold in dried beef and pecans. Refrigerate. Yields 1 pint.

Chunky Shrimp Dip

2 (6 ounce) cans shrimp, drained
2 cups mayonnaise

6 green onions, finely chopped
¾ cup chunky salsa

- Crumble shrimp and stir in mayonnaise, onion and salsa in bowl.
- Refrigerate for 1 to 2 hours. Yields 1½ pints.

Party Shrimp Dip

1 (8 ounce) package cream
  cheese, softened
½ cup mayonnaise

1 (6 ounce) can tiny, cooked
  shrimp, drained
¾ teaspoon Creole seasoning

- Beat cream cheese and mayonnaise in bowl. Stir in shrimp and seasoning.
- Mix well and refrigerate. Yields 1 pint.

Easy Tuna Dip

1 (6 ounce) can tuna, drained
1 (1 ounce) packet Italian salad
  dressing mix

1 (8 ounce) carton sour cream
2 green onions with tops,
  chopped

- Combine all ingredients in bowl and mix well. Refrigerate for several hours before serving. Yields 1½ cups.

Cheesy Crab Dip

1 (6 ounce) roll garlic cheese,
  diced
1 (10 ounce) can cream of
  mushroom soup

1 (6 ounce) can crabmeat,
  drained, flaked
2 tablespoons sherry

- Heat all ingredients in medium saucepan and stir until cheese melts.
- Keep warm in chafing dish. Yields 1 pint.

Unbelievable Crab Dip

1 (6 ounce) can white crabmeat, drained, flaked

1 (8 ounce) package cream cheese
½ cup (1 stick) butter

- Combine crabmeat, cream cheese and butter in saucepan.
- Heat, stir constantly until thoroughly mixed. Transfer to chafing dish. Yields 1½ cups.

Fast Clam Dip

1 (1 ounce) packet onion soup mix
1 (16 ounce) carton sour cream

1 (7 ounce) can minced clams, drained
2 tablespoons chili sauce

- Combine onion soup mix and sour cream in bowl and mix well.
- Add clams and chili sauce. Mix well and refrigerate. Yields 1 pint.

Speedy Gonzales

1 (16 ounce) package cubed processed American cheese
½ cup milk

1 (12 ounce) jar salsa, divided
Tortilla chips

- Melt cheese and milk in double boiler.
- Add about half salsa. Serve with tortilla chips. Yields 1½ pints.

Tip: Add more salsa for extra heat.

Speedy Cheese Dip

2 (10 ounce) cans cheddar cheese
soup
1 (10 ounce) can diced tomatoes
and green chilies

1 (10 ounce) can cream of chicken
soup
Pinch of cayenne pepper

- Mix all ingredients in saucepan.

- Serve hot with chips. Yields 2½ cups.

Black Olive Spread

1 (8 ounce) package cream
cheese, softened
½ cup mayonnaise
1 (4 ounce) can chopped black
olives, drained

3 fresh green onions, chopped
very fine

- Beat cream cheese and mayonnaise in bowl until smooth.

- Add olives and onions and refrigerate. Yields 1 pint.

Simple Veggie Dip

1 (10 ounce) package frozen,
chopped spinach, thawed, well
drained
1 (16 ounce) carton sour cream

1 (1 ounce) packet vegetable
soup mix
1 bunch fresh green onions with
tops, chopped

- Squeeze spinach between paper towels to completely remove
excess moisture.

- Combine all ingredients in glass bowl. Refrigerate for several
hours before serving. Yields 1½ pints.

Tangy Artichoke Mix ～～～～～～～～

½ cup (1 stick) butter
1 (14 ounce) can artichoke hearts,
   drained, chopped

1 (4 ounce) carton crumbled
   blue cheese
2 teaspoons lemon juice

- Melt butter in skillet and mix in artichoke hearts.
- Add blue cheese and lemon juice. Serve hot. Yields 1½ cups.

Holy Guacamole ～～～～～～～～

4 avocados, peeled
½ cup salsa

¼ cup sour cream
Tortilla chips

- Split avocados and remove seeds. Mash avocado with fork in bowl.
- Add salsa and sour cream. Serve with tortilla chips. Yields 1 pint.

Broccoli-Cheese Dip ～～～～～～～～

1 (10 ounce) can broccoli-cheese
   soup
1 (10 ounce) package frozen,
   chopped broccoli, thawed

½ cup sour cream
2 teaspoons of dijon-style
   mustard

- Combine soup, broccoli, sour cream and mustard in saucepan and mix well.
- Heat and serve hot. Yields 1½ pints.

Sassy Onion Dip

1 (8 ounce) package cream
   cheese, softened
1 (8 ounce) carton sour cream

½ cup chili sauce
1 (1 ounce) packet onion soup
   mix

- Beat cream cheese in bowl until fluffy.

- Add remaining ingredients and mix well.

- Cover and refrigerate. Yields 1½ cups.

Spinach-Artichoke Dip

2 (10 ounce) boxes frozen spinach,
   thawed, drained
1 (14 ounce) jar marinated
   artichoke hearts, drained,
   finely chopped

1 cup mayonnaise
1 (8 ounce) package shredded
   mozzarella cheese

- Squeeze spinach between paper towels to remove excess moisture.

- Combine spinach, artichoke hearts, mayonnaise and cheese
  in bowl and mix well.

- Cover and refrigerate. Yields 1 quart.

SALTY SOUP? IF YOUR SAUCE, SOUP OR STEW IS TOO SALTY, ADD A PEELED POTATO TO THE POT, AND IT WILL ABSORB THE EXTRA SALT.

Soups, Salads and Sandwiches

Cream of Turkey Soup

1 (10 ounce) can cream of celery
    soup
1 (10 ounce) can cream of
    chicken soup

2 soup cans milk
1 cup cooked, finely diced
    turkey

- Combine all ingredients in large saucepan and serve hot.
  Serves 4.

Spicy Tomato Soup

2 (10 ounce) cans tomato soup
1 (15 ounce) can Mexican stewed
    tomatoes

Sour cream
½ pound bacon, fried, drained,
    crumbled

- Combine soup and stewed tomatoes in saucepan and heat.
- To serve, place dollop of sour cream on each bowl of soup and
  sprinkle crumbled bacon over sour cream. Serves 4.

Super Supper Gumbo

1 (10 ounce) can pepper pot soup
1 (10 ounce) can chicken gumbo
  soup
1 (6 ounce) can white crabmeat,

flaked
1 (6 ounce) can tiny shrimp,
  drained

- Combine all ingredients with 1½ soup cans water in saucepan.

- Cover and simmer for 15 minutes. Serves 4.

Chicken Caesar Salad

4 boneless, skinless chicken
  breast halves, grilled
1 (10 ounce) package romaine
  salad greens

½ cup shredded parmesan
  cheese
¾ cup Caesar or Italian
  dressing

- Cut chicken breasts into strips. Combine chicken, salad greens and cheese in large bowl.

- When ready to serve, toss with dressing. Serves 6.

Derby Chicken Salad

3–4 boneless skinless chicken
  breast halves, cooked, cubed
2 avocados, peeled, diced

2 tomatoes, diced, drained
Italian salad dressing

- Combine all ingredients in bowl.

- When ready to serve, pour dressing over salad and toss.
  Refrigerate. Serves 6.

Select Spinach Salad

1 (10 ounce) package fresh
   spinach
2 eggs, hard-boiled, sliced

1 (14 ounce) can bean sprouts,
   drained
1 (11 ounce) can sliced water
   chestnuts, chopped

- Combine all salad ingredients in large bowl. Serves 4.

Broccoli-Pepperoni Crunch

1 (1 pound) bunch broccoli
½ pound fresh mushrooms, sliced

1 (3 ounce) package sliced
   pepperoni, chopped
Italian dressing

- Cut off broccoli florets. Combine broccoli, mushrooms, cheese and pepperoni in bowl. Toss with Italian dressing.

- Refrigerate for at least 8 hours before serving. Serves 4.

Tip: Adding ¾ cup diced Swiss cheese gives this salad more color and texture, but it is not mandatory. This is great just like it is.

Red Cabbage Slaw

1 large head red cabbage
2 onions, finely chopped

½ cup coleslaw dressing
½ cup French salad dressing

- Slice cabbage and combine with onions in bowl.

- In separate bowl, combine dressings and toss with cabbage and onions. Refrigerate. Serves 4.

Hometown Deviled Eggs

6 eggs, hard-boiled
2 tablespoons sweet pickle relish

3 tablespoons mayonnaise
½ teaspoon mustard

- Peel eggs and cut in half lengthwise. Take yolks and mash with fork in bowl.

- Add relish, mayonnaise and mustard to yolks. Place yolk mixture back into egg white halves. Yields 12.

Tip: Some people like to sprinkle paprika over deviled eggs to give them color.

Creamy Cranberry Salad

1 (6 ounce) package cherry
   gelatin
1 (8 ounce) carton sour cream

1 (16 ounce) can whole cranberry
   sauce
1 (8 ounce) can crushed
   pineapple with liquid

- Dissolve gelatin in 1 cup boiling water in bowl and mix well.

- Stir in remaining ingredients and pour into 7 x 11-inch glass dish.

- Refrigerate until firm. Serves 8.

SPANISH COLONISTS INTRODUCED TO NORTH AMERICA ALMONDS, APPLES, APRICOTS, BANANAS, BARLEY, BEANS, CHERRIES, CHICKPEAS, CHILIES, CITRONS, DATES, FIGS, GRAPES, LEMONS, LENTILS, LIMES, MAIZE, OLIVES, NECTARINES, ORANGES, PEACHES, PEARS, PLUMS, POMEGRANATES, QUINCES, TOMATIAS, WALNUTS, WHEAT, CHICKENS, COWS, DONKEYS, GOATS, HORSES, SHEEP AND DOMESTICATED TURKEY. SPANISH COLONISTS ALSO INTRODUCED SAFFRON, OLIVE OIL AND ANISE.

Ranch-Style Cheeseburgers

1 (1 ounce) packet ranch salad
    dressing mix
1 pound lean ground beef

1 cup shredded cheddar cheese
4 large hamburger buns, toasted

- Combine dressing mix with beef and cheese in bowl. Shape into 4 patties.

- Cook on charcoal grill until they thoroughly cook and brown. Serve on hamburger buns. Serves 4.

Hot Bunwiches

8 hamburger buns
8 slices Swiss cheese

8 slices ham
8 slices turkey

- Lay out all 8 buns. On bottom bun, place slices of Swiss cheese, ham and turkey.

- Place top bun over turkey. Wrap each bunwich individually in foil and place in freezer.

- When ready to serve, take out of freezer 2 to 3 hours before serving. Preheat oven to 325° and heat for about 30 minutes and serve hot. Serves 8.

Tip: If you want it extra cheesy, add another slice of cheese, any kind.

CHEESE MAY BE FROZEN. PROCESSED CHEESES WILL LAST 4 MONTHS FROZEN AND CHEDDAR OR OTHER NATURAL CHEESES WILL KEEP ABOUT 6 WEEKS WHEN PROPERLY WRAPPED. THAW ALL CHEESE OVERNIGHT IN REFRIGERATOR AND USE SOON AFTER THAWING.

Main Dishes: Chicken

Golden Chicken

> 6 boneless, skinless chicken
>   breast halves
> ¼ cup (½ stick) butter
>
> 1(10 ounce) can golden
>   mushroom soup
> ½ cup sliced almonds

- Preheat oven to 350°.
- Place chicken breasts in sprayed 9 x 13-inch baking pan.
- Combine butter, soup, almonds and ¼ cup water in saucepan. Heat and mix just until butter melts.
- Pour mixture over chicken. Cover and bake for 1 hour. Serves 6.

Chicken Crunch

> 4–6 boneless, skinless chicken
>   breast halves
> ½ cup Italian salad dressing
>
> ½ cup sour cream
> 2½ cups crushed corn flakes

- Place chicken in resealable plastic bag and add salad dressing and sour cream. Seal and refrigerate for 1 hour.
- When ready to bake, preheat oven to 375°.
- Remove chicken from marinade and discard marinade.
- Dredge chicken in corn flakes and place in sprayed 9 x 13-inch baking dish.
- Bake for 45 minutes. Serves 6.

Chicken Delight ～～～～～～～～～

6 boneless, skinless chicken
   breast halves

1 (8 ounce) carton whipped cream
   cheese with onion and chives
Butter, softened
6 bacon strips

- Preheat oven to 375°.

- Flatten chicken to ½-inch thickness. Spread 3 tablespoons cream cheese over each.

- Dot with butter and roll. Wrap each with bacon strip.

- Place seam-side down in sprayed 9 x 13-inch baking dish.

- Bake for 40 to 45 minutes or until juices run clear.

- To brown, broil 6 inches from heat for about 3 minutes or until bacon is crisp. Serves 6.

Saucy Chicken ～～～～～～～～

5–6 boneless, skinless chicken
   breast halves
2 cups thick-and-chunky salsa

$^1/_3$ cup packed light brown sugar
1½ tablespoons dijon-style
   mustard

- Preheat oven to 350°.

- Place chicken breasts in sprayed 9 x 13-inch baking dish.

- Combine salsa, brown sugar and mustard in bowl and pour over chicken.

- Cover and bake for 45 minutes. Serves 6.

Tip: This tastes great served over cooked rice.

Mushroom Chicken with Wine

6–8 boneless, skinless chicken
  breast halves
1 (10 ounce) can cream of
  mushroom soup

1 (10 ounce) can cream of onion
  soup
1 cup white wine

- Preheat oven to 325°.

- Brown chicken in sprayed skillet. Place in 10 x 15-inch baking dish.

- Combine soups and wine in bowl and pour over chicken.

- Cover and bake for 35 minutes. Uncover and bake for additional
  25 minutes. Serves 8.

Asparagus Chicken

1 (1 ounce) packet hollandaise
  sauce mix
2 large boneless, skinless chicken
  breasts, cut into strips

1 (15 ounce) can asparagus
  spears
1 (8 ounce) package wide
  noodles

- Prepare hollandaise sauce according to package directions.

- Cook chicken strips in large skillet for 12 to 15 minutes or until brown
  and stir occasionally. Add hollandaise sauce and lemon juice.

- Cover and cook for additional 10 minutes and stir occasionally.

- When ready to serve, place chicken strips over noodles and top
  with heated asparagus spears. Serves 6.

Pineapple-Glazed Chicken

4 boneless, skinless chicken
breast halves, cubed
1 (15 ounce) can pineapple chunks
with juice
½ cup honey mustard grill-and-
glaze sauce
1 red bell pepper, seeded,
chopped

- Brown chicken in skillet and cook on low heat for 15 minutes.
  Add pineapple, honey mustard and bell pepper.

- Bring to a boil, reduce heat to low and simmer for 10 to 15 minutes
  or until sauce thickens slightly. Serves 4.

Tip: This chicken is wonderful over cooked rice.

Rosemary Chicken

½ cup flour
1 tablespoon dried rosemary,
divided
Italian dressing
3–5 boneless, skinless chicken
breast halves

- Preheat oven to 350°.

- Combine flour and half rosemary in bowl. In separate shallow
  bowl, pour a little Italian dressing and dip chicken breasts
  in dressing.

- Dredge chicken in flour mixture. Place in sprayed 9 x 13-inch
  shallow baking dish.

- Bake for 40 minutes. Remove from oven and sprinkle remaining
  rosemary over breasts and cook for an additional 10 minutes.
  Serves 3 to 5.

REDUCED-SODIUM, REDUCED-FAT
CHICKEN BROTH WORKS JUST AS WELL
AS CHICKEN BROTH AND HELPS LOWER
ONE'S SODIUM INTAKE.

Chicken Dipsticks

1½ cups cornbread stuffing mix
4 tablespoons olive oil

4 boneless, skinless chicken
breast halves
Chicken Dipsticks Sauce

- Preheat oven to 350°.
- Place stuffing mix in resealable plastic bag and crush with rolling pin.
- Add oil to center of 9 x 13-inch baking pan and spread around entire pan.
- Cut chicken breasts into 3 or 4 pieces, dip in stuffing mix and place in baking pan. Arrange chicken making sure pieces are not touching.
- Bake for 25 minutes. Remove from oven, turn pieces over and bake for additional 15 minutes or until brown. Serves 4.

Chicken Dipsticks Sauce:

¼ cup honey

3 tablespoons spicy brown
mustard

- Combine honey and brown mustard in bowl. Serve chicken with sauce and enjoy. Yields ⅓ cup.

Crispy Nutty Chicken ~~~~~~~

⅓ cup minced dry roasted
peanuts
1 cup corn flake crumbs

½ cup ranch buttermilk salad
dressing
5–6 chicken breast halves

- Preheat oven to 350°.

- Combine peanuts and corn flake crumbs on wax paper. Pour salad dressing into pie pan.

- Dip each piece chicken in salad dressing and roll in crumb mixture to coat.

- Arrange chicken in sprayed 9 x 13-inch shallow baking dish.

- Bake for 50 minutes until light brown. Serves 5 to 6.

Apricot-Ginger Chicken ~~~~~~~

2 teaspoons ground ginger
¾ cup Italian dressing

4 boneless, skinless chicken
breast halves
⅔ cup apricot preserves

- Combine ginger and Italian dressing; set aside ¼ cup. Place remaining dressing in large resealable plastic bag.

- Add chicken to bag and marinate in refrigerator overnight; turn occasionally.

- When ready to bake, preheat oven to 350°.

- When ready to cook, remove chicken and place in sprayed 9 x 13-inch baking dish.

- Pour ¼ cup marinade in saucepan, bring to a boil and cook for 1 minute. Remove from heat, stir in preserves and set aside.

- Bake chicken for 45 minutes and brush with cooked marinade mixture last 10 minutes of cooking. Serves 4.

Bacon-Wrapped Chicken

1 (4 ounce) jar sliced dried beef, separated
6 strips bacon
6 boneless, skinless chicken breast halves
1 (10 ounce) can cream of chicken soup

- Preheat oven to 325°.

- Place dried beef in sprayed 9 x 13-inch baking dish. Wrap bacon strip around each chicken breast half and place over beef.

- Heat soup and ¼ cup water in saucepan and pour over chicken.

- Cover and bake for 1 hour 10 minutes. Serves 6.

Mozzarella Cutlets

4 boneless, skinless chicken breast halves
1 cup Italian seasoned dry breadcrumbs, divided
1 cup prepared spaghetti sauce
4 slices mozzarella cheese

- Preheat oven to 350°.

- Pound each chicken breast to flatten slightly.

- Coat chicken well in breadcrumbs. Arrange chicken breasts in sprayed 9 x 13-inch baking dish.

- Place quarter of sauce over each portion. Place 1 slice cheese over each and garnish with remaining breadcrumbs.

- Bake for 45 minutes. Serves 4.

PEANUT OIL IS CONSIDERED ONE OF THE BEST OILS FOR FRYING BECAUSE IT HAS A VERY HIGH SMOKE POINT. THE OIL CAN REACH HIGHER TEMPERATURES THAN MOST OILS BEFORE IT BEGINS TO SMOKE. PEANUT OIL DOES NOT ABSORB OR TRANSFER FLAVORS, SO THE SAME OIL IS USED FOR DIFFERENT FOODS WITHOUT IT AFFECTING THE TASTE OF THE FOODS.

Jiffy Chicken

6 boneless, skinless chicken
    breast halves
¾ cup mayonnaise

2 cups crushed corn flake crumbs
½ cup grated parmesan cheese

- Preheat oven to 325°.

- Dip chicken in mayonnaise and spread mayonnaise over chicken with brush.

- Combine corn flakes and parmesan cheese in bowl. Dip mayonnaise-covered chicken in corn flake mixture. Get plenty of crumbs on chicken.

- Place in sprayed 9 x 13-inch glass baking dish. Bake for 1 hour. Serves 6.

Skillet Chicken and Stuffing

1 (6 ounce) box stuffing mix for
    chicken
1 (16 ounce) package frozen whole
    kernel corn

¼ cup (½ stick) butter
4 boneless, skinless chicken
    breast halves, cooked

- Combine contents of seasoning packet in stuffing mix, corn, 1⅔ cups water and butter in large skillet.

- Bring to a boil. Reduce heat, cover and simmer for 5 minutes.

- Stir in stuffing mix just until moist. Cut chicken into thin slices. Mix with stuffing-corn mixture.

- Cook on low heat just until thoroughly hot. Serves 4.

Quick-Fix Chicken Supper

5 boneless, skinless chicken
   breast halves
5 slices onion

5 potatoes, peeled, quartered
1 (10 ounce) can cream of celery
   soup

- Preheat oven to 325°.

- Place chicken breasts in sprayed 9 x 13-inch baking dish. Top chicken with onion slices and place potatoes around chicken.

- Heat soup with ¼ cup water in saucepan just enough to pour soup over chicken and vegetables.

- Cover and bake for 1 hour 10 minutes. Serves 5.

Sesame Chicken

½ cup (1 stick) butter, melted
¾ tablespoon chili powder
4 boneless, skinless chicken
   breast halves

1 cup sesame seeds, lightly
   toasted

- Preheat oven to 325°.

- Combine butter and chili powder in bowl.

- Dip chicken in butter mixture and roll in sesame seeds.

- Place in sprayed 9 x 13- inch baking dish. Bake for 1 hour and turn after 30 minutes. Serves 4.

Main Dishes: Beef

Best Ever Meatloaf

2 pounds ground turkey
1 (6 ounce) package stuffing mix
   for chicken

2 eggs, beaten
½ cup ketchup, divided

- Preheat oven to 350°.

- Combine ground turkey, stuffing mix, eggs and ¼ cup ketchup in bowl and mix well.

- Shape meat into oval loaf and palce in center of 9 x 13-inch baking dish.

- Spread remaining ¼ cup ketchup on top of loaf.

- Bake for 1 hour. Serves 8.

Southwestern Steak

1 pound tenderized round steak
Flour
1 (15 ounce) can Mexican stewed
   tomatoes

2 teaspoons beef bouillon
   granules

- Preheat oven to 325°.

- Cut beef into serving-size pieces and dredge in flour. Brown steak in sprayed skillet.

- Mix tomatoes and beef bouillon in bowl and pour over steak.

- Cover and bake for 1 hour. Serves 6.

Baked Onion-Mushroom Steak

1½ pounds (½ inch thick) round
   steak
1 (10 ounce) can cream of
mushroom soup
1 (1 ounce) packet onion soup
   mix

- Preheat oven to 325°.

- Place steak in sprayed 9 x 13-inch baking dish.

- Combine mushroom soup and ½ cup water in bowl and pour over steak and sprinkle with onion soup mix.

- Cover and bake for 2 hours. Serves 8.

Round Steak Sizzle

2 pounds (½ inch thick) round
   steak
Olive oil
1 onion, thinly sliced
2 (10 ounce) cans tomato bisque
   soup

- Cut steak into serving-size pieces. Brown meat in a little oil in skillet.

- Mix onion and soup with 1 soup can water in bowl and add to steak. Bring to a boil.

- Turn heat down, cover and simmer for 1 hour 20 minutes. Serves 8.

*Tip: If you want a little breading on the meat,
dust meat with flour and a little salt and
pepper before browning in skillet.*

Red Wine Round Steak ~~~~~~~

2 pounds (¾ inch thick) round
   steak
1 (1 ounce) packet onion soup mix

1 cup dry red wine
1 (4 ounce) can sliced
   mushrooms

- Preheat oven to 325°.

- Remove all fat from steak and cut in serving-size pieces.
  Brown meat on both sides in sprayed skillet. Place in sprayed
  9 x 13-inch baking dish.

- Combine onion soup mix, wine, 1 cup hot water and mushrooms in
  skillet. Pour over browned steak.

- Cover and bake for 1 hour 20 minutes or until steak is tender.
  Serves 8 to 10.

Smothered Steak Break ~~~~~~~

1 large round steak
1 (10 ounce) can golden mushroom
   soup

1 (1 ounce) packet onion soup
   mix
⅔ cup milk

- Preheat oven to 325°.

- Cut steak into serving-size pieces and place in sprayed
  9 x 13-inch baking pan.

- Mix soup, dry onion soup and milk in saucepan. Heat just enough
  to mix well. Pour over steak.

- Seal with foil. Bake for 1 hour. Serves 6.

Beef-Broccoli Stack

1 pound beef sirloin steak
1 onion, chopped
1 (10 ounce) can cream of broccoli
  soup

1 (10 ounce) package frozen
  chopped broccoli, thawed

- Slice beef across grain into very thin strips. Brown steak strips and onion in large sprayed skillet and stir several times.

- Add a little water, reduce heat and simmer for 10 minutes. Mix in soup and broccoli and heat. Serves 4.

Tip: *Try this over noodles. It's great. The flavors mix really well and the noodles soak it all up.*

Creamy Mushroom Beef

2 (10 ounce) cans golden
  mushroom soup
½ cup cooking sherry

1 (1 ounce) packet onion soup mix
2 pounds lean beef, cubed

- Preheat oven to 325°.

- Mix soup, sherry and onion soup mix with ¾ cup water in bowl.

- Add steak cubes to sprayed 3-quart baking dish and pour soup mixture on top.

- Bake for about 2 hours. Serves 8 to 10.

Tip: *The creamy gravy with this beef is excellent over noodles, rice or toasted bread.*

Savory Rib Roast

1 tablespoon dried thyme
1 tablespoon dried, crushed
  rosemary
1 teaspoon rubbed sage
1 (4–5 pound) boneless beef roast

- Preheat oven to 350°.

- Combine thyme, rosemary and sage in small bowl and rub over roast. Place roast, fat-side up.

- Bake on rack in large roasting pan for 2 hours to 2 hours 30 minutes or until meat reaches desired doneness.

- Remove roast to warm serving platter and let stand for 10 minutes before slicing. Serves 8 to 10.

Tender Beef Roast

1 (3–4) pound rump roast
1 (10 ounce) can French onion
  soup
1 (14 ounce) can beef bouillon
1 teaspoon garlic powder

- Preheat oven to 325°.

- Place roast in sprayed roasting pan. Pour soup and bouillon over roast and sprinkle with garlic powder.

- Place lid on roasting pan and bake for 3 hours 30 minutes. Pour pan gravy over roast after it's sliced. Serves 8.

Simple Chuck Roast Meal

1 (3–4 pound) boneless rump roast or chuck roast
4 medium potatoes, peeled, cut into pieces

2 onions, quartered
1 (10 ounce) can golden mushroom soup

- Preheat oven to 350°.
- Place seasoned* meat in roasting pan with 1 cup water. Cover and bake for about 1 hour.
- Uncover, add potatoes and onions and continue cooking for additional 1 hour.
- Combine soup and ½ cup water in saucepan. Heat just enough to pour over roast and vegetables.
- Place roaster back in oven just until soup is hot. Serves 8.

*Tip: Everyone seasons food according to their tastes. Salt and pepper work great for this roast. Lemon pepper, garlic salt or seasoned salt are excellent. Season with whatever you have.

Easy Breezy Brisket

1 (4–5 pound) brisket
1 (1 ounce) packet onion soup mix

2 tablespoons Worcestershire sauce
1 cup red wine

- Preheat oven to 325°.
- Place brisket in shallow baking pan. Sprinkle onion soup mix over brisket.
- Pour Worcestershire sauce and red wine in baking pan. Cover and bake for 5 to 6 hours. Serves 8.

Slow Cookin' Brisket

½ cup liquid hickory-flavored
smoke
1 (4–5 pound) beef brisket

1 (5 ounce) bottle Worcestershire
sauce
¾ cup barbecue sauce

- Pour liquid smoke over brisket. Cover and refrigerate overnight.

- When ready to bake, preheat oven to 275°.

- Drain and pour Worcestershire sauce over brisket. Cover and bake
  for 6 to 7 hours.

- Uncover and pour barbecue sauce over brisket and bake for
  additional 30 minutes. Slice very thin across grain. Serves 8.

Taste-of-the-Irish Corned Beef

1 (4–5) pound corned beef brisket
4 large potatoes, peeled,
quartered

6 carrots, peeled, halved
1 head cabbage

- Place corned beef in roasting pan, cover with water and bring
  to a boil. Turn heat down and simmer for 3 hours. Add water
  if necessary.

- Add potatoes and carrots. Cut cabbage into eighths and lay
  over top of other vegetables.

- Bring to a boil, turn heat down and cook for additional 30 to
  40 minutes or until vegetables are done. When slightly cool,
  slice corned beef across grain. Serves 8.

Potato-Beef Bake ~~~~~~~~~~~~~~~~

1 pound ground beef
1 (10 ounce) can sloppy Joe sauce
1 (10 ounce) can fiesta nacho
  cheese soup

1 (32 ounce) package frozen hash-
  brown potatoes, thawed

- Preheat oven to 400°.

- Cook beef in skillet over medium heat until no longer pink
  and drain.

- Add sloppy Joe sauce and fiesta nacho cheese soup.

- Place hash browns in sprayed 9 x 13-inch baking dish. Top
  with beef mixture.

- Cover and bake for 25 minutes. Uncover and bake for additional 10
  minutes. Serves 6.

*Tip: If you really like a cheesy dish, sprinkle shredded cheddar
cheese on top just before serving.*

Meat and Potato Stew ~~~~~~~~~~~~~~

2 pounds beef stew meat
2 (15 ounce) cans new potatoes,
  drained

1 (15 ounce) can sliced carrots,
  drained
1 (10 ounce) can French onion
  soup

- Cook stew meat with about 2 cups water in large pot for 1 hour
  over medium heat.

- Add potatoes, carrots and onion soup and mix. Bring to a boil,
  reduce heat and simmer for 30 minutes or until potatoes are
  tender. Serves 6 to 8.

Main Dishes: Pork

Plum Peachy Pork Roast

1 (4–5 pound) boneless pork loin
  roast
1 (12 ounce) jar plum jelly

½ cup peach preserves
½ teaspoon ginger

- Preheat oven to 325°.
- Place roast in shallow baking pan and bake for 1 hour.
- Turn roast to brown and bake for additional 1 hour.
- Heat jelly, peach preserves and ginger in saucepan. Brush roast generously with preserve mixture after it is done.
- Bake for an additional 15 minutes and baste again.
- Serve preserve mixture and liquid in baking pan with roast. Serves 6.

Hawaiian Pork Tenderloin

1 (2 pound) lean pork tenderloin,
  cut in 1-inch cubes
1 (15 ounce) can pineapple chunks

  with liquid
1 (12 ounce) bottle chili sauce
1 teaspoon ground ginger

- Place all ingredients in skillet.
- Cover and simmer for 1 hour 30 minutes. Serves 8.

Tenderloin with Apricot Sauce

3 pounds pork tenderloin
1 cup apricot preserves

$^1/_3$ cup lemon juice
$^1/_3$ cup ketchup

- Preheat oven to 325°.

- Place tenderloin in sprayed roasting pan. Combine preserves, lemon juice and ketchup in bowl and pour over pork.

- Cover and bake for 1 hour 20 minutes. Baste once during cooking. Serves 6.

*Tip: This tenderloin is great with the apricot sauce.
If you want to serve a heartier dish, add rice
and serve tenderloin on top.*

Apple-Topped Tenderloin

1½ cups hickory marinade,
   divided
1 (3–4 pound) pork tenderloin

1 (20 ounce) can apple pie filling
¾ teaspoon ground cinnamon

- Combine 1 cup marinade and tenderloin in resealable plastic bag. Marinate in refrigerator for at least 1 hour.

- When ready to cook, preheat oven to 325°.

- Remove tenderloin and discard used marinade.

- Cook tenderloin for 1 hour and baste twice with ¼ cup marinade. Let stand for 10 or 15 minutes before slicing.

- Combine pie filling, remaining ¼ cup marinade and cinnamon in saucepan and heat. Serve sauce over sliced tenderloin. Serves 8.

Honey-Ham Slice ~~~~~~~~~

¹/₃ cup orange juice
¹/₃ cup honey
1 teaspoon mustard

1 (1 inch thick) slice fully cooked
ham

- Combine orange juice, honey and mustard in saucepan, cook slowly for 10 minutes and stir occasionally.

- Brush ham with orange glaze. Place in broiling pan about 3 inches from heat.

- Broil for 8 minutes on first side. Turn ham slice over. Brush with glaze again and broil for additional 6 to 8 minutes. Serves 4.

Tempting Mustard Ham ~~~~~~~

1 (1 inch thick) slice cooked ham
2 teaspoons dry mustard

¹/₃ cup honey
¹/₃ cup cooking wine

- Preheat oven to 350°.

- Rub ham slice with 1 teaspoon mustard on each side. Place in shallow baking pan.

- Combine honey and wine in bowl and pour over ham. Bake for about 35 minutes. Serves 4.

Piggy Pork Picante ~~~~~~~~

1 pound pork tenderloin, cubed
1 (1 ounce) packet taco seasoning

1 cup chunky salsa
¹/₃ cup peach preserves

- Toss pork with taco seasoning and brown in skillet.

- Stir in salsa and preserves. Bring to a boil.

- Lower heat and simmer for 30 minutes. Serves 4.

Tangy Pork Chops

4–6 pork chops
¼ cup Worcestershire sauce

¼ cup ketchup
½ cup honey

- Preheat oven to 325°.

- Brown pork chops in skillet. Place in shallow baking dish.

- Combine Worcestershire sauce, ketchup and honey in bowl. Pour over pork chops.

- Cover and bake for 45 minutes. Serves 4 to 6.

Sweet and Savory Pork Chops

4–6 (1 inch thick) boneless pork
   chops, trimmed
½ cup grape, apple or plum jelly

½ cup chili sauce or hot ketchup
Soy sauce or teriyaki sauce

- Preheat oven to 325°.

- Brown pork chops in skillet. Transfer browned pork chops to shallow baking dish.

- Combine jelly and chili sauce or ketchup in bowl and spread over pork chops.

- Bake for 15 minutes, baste with sauce and Bake for additional 15 minutes or until pork chops are tender. Serve with soy sauce or teriyaki sauce. Serves 4 to 6.

Apple Pork Chops

4 butterflied pork chops
2 apples, peeled, cored

2 teaspoons butter
2 tablespoons brown sugar

- Preheat oven to 350°.

- Place pork chops in sprayed shallow baking dish.

- Cover and bake for 30 minutes. Uncover and place apple halves on top of pork chops. Add a little butter and a little brown sugar on each apple.

- Bake for additional 15 minutes. Serves 4.

Tip: Seasoning is always up to you, but salt and pepper are probably plenty for these pork chops.

Spicy Pork Chops

4–6 pork chops
1 large onion
1 bell pepper, seeded

1 (10 ounce) can diced tomatoes
and green chilies

- Preheat oven to 350°.

- Brown pork chops in sprayed skillet. Place chops in sprayed baking dish.

- Cut onion and bell pepper into large chunks and place on chops. Pour tomatoes and green chilies over chops.

- Cover and bake for 45 minutes. Serves 4 to 6.

Barbecued Spareribs ~~~~~~~~~~

3–4 pounds pork spareribs
   or country-style pork ribs,
   trimmed
1 cup hot ketchup or chili sauce

½ cup honey or packed brown
   sugar
1 teaspoon liquid smoke

- Preheat oven to 350°.

- Place spareribs on sprayed broiler pan and bake for 1 hour 30 minutes

- Combine ketchup, honey or brown sugar and liquid smoke in small saucepan and simmer for 2 to 3 minutes.

- Baste spareribs generously on both sides with ketchup mixture.

- Reduce heat to 300°. Bake for additional 1 hour 30 minutes or until tender; baste generously every 15 to 20 minutes. Serves 4.

Sweet-and-Sour Spareribs ~~~~~~~~~~

4 pounds pork spareribs
1 (6 ounce) can frozen lemonade
   concentrate, thawed

½ teaspoon garlic salt
⅓ cup soy sauce

- Preheat oven to 350°.

- Place spareribs, meaty-side down in shallow, sprayed roasting pan with a little water. Cover and cook for 40 minutes.

- Remove cover, drain fat and return ribs to oven. Bake for additional 30 minutes. Drain fat again.

- Combine remaining ingredients in bowl and brush on ribs.

- Reduce temperature to 325°. Cover and bake for 1 hour or until tender and brush occasionally with sauce. Serves 4 to 6.

Main Dishes: Seafood

Crispy Flounder

⅓ cup mayonnaise
1 pound flounder fillets

1 cup seasoned breadcrumbs
¼ cup grated parmesan cheese

- Preheat oven to 375°.
- Place mayonnaise in small dish. Coat fish with mayonnaise and dip in breadcrumbs to coat well.
- Arrange in sprayed 9 x 13-inch baking dish and cover with parmesan cheese. Bake for 15 to 20 minutes. Serves 2 to 4.

Fried Haddock Fillets

1½ cups lemon-lime soda
1 pound haddock fillets

2 cups biscuit mix
Olive oil

- Pour soda in shallow bowl, add fillets and marinate for 15 minutes.
- In separate shallow bowl, combine biscuit mix. Remove fish from soda and coat with biscuit mix.
- Heat about ¼-inch oil in large skillet. Fry fish for about 3 minutes on each side or until fish flakes with fork. Drain on paper towels. Serves 6.

Fish and Chips

1 cup mayonnaise
2 tablespoons fresh lime juice

3–4 fish fillets, rinsed, dried
1½ cups crushed corn chips

- Preheat oven to 425°.

- Mix mayonnaise and lime juice in bowl. Spread on both sides of fish fillets.

- Place crushed corn chips on wax paper and dredge both sides of fish in crushed chips. Shake off excess chips.

- Place fillets on foil-covered baking sheet and bake for 15 minutes or until fish flakes. Serve with lime wedges. Serves 4.

Red Fish Barbecue

2 pounds red fish fillets
1 (8 ounce) bottle Italian dressing

1 (12 ounce) can beer
Several dashes hot sauce

- Place fish in glass baking dish. Pour Italian dressing, beer and hot sauce over fish.

- Cover and marinate in refrigerator for at least 2 hours.

- When ready to cook, drain fish, discard marinade and place in microwave-safe dish.

- Microwave fish for about 2 to 4 minutes per pound. Serves 4 to 6.

Butter-Baked Fish Fillets ∼∼∼∼∼∼∼

½ cup (1 stick) butter
4–6 cod or flounder fillets

Lemon juice

- Preheat oven to 400°.

- Place butter in shallow baking dish in very hot oven until it melts and browns slightly.

- Place fillets in hot butter and cook for 10 minutes. Turn and baste with pan juices. Sprinkle fish with lemon juice.

- Bake for additional few minutes or until fish flakes easily. Serves 4.

Simple Summer Shrimp Supper ∼∼∼∼∼∼

1½ pounds cooked, peeled shrimp
1 small head lettuce, chopped

1 (14 ounce) jar artichokes,
    quartered, drained
1 avocado, sliced

- Combine all ingredients in bowl. Serve 4.

Tip: This shrimp supper is great just as it is, but if you
    want cocktail or a creamy dressing, just add it.
    You don't need it, but some people like shrimp
    with some kind of dressing.

Broiled Salmon Steaks

4 (1 inch thick) salmon steaks
Garlic salt

Worcestershire sauce
¼–½ cup butter, melted

- Place salmon steaks on sprayed baking sheet and sprinkle both sides with garlic salt.

- Splash Worcestershire sauce and butter on top of each salmon steak and broil for 2 to 3 minutes.

- Remove from oven and turn each steak. Splash more Worcestershire sauce and butter on top and broil for 2 to 3 more minutes.

- Top with a little melted butter just before serving. Serves 4.

Tip: It's easy to cook fish too long. Just make sure it is still moist inside, not dry on the outside and flakes as you pull meat apart with fork.

Scrumptious Salmon Bites

1 (15 ounce) can pink salmon with liquid
1 egg

½ cup cracker crumbs
1 teaspoon baking powder

- Drain salmon and set aside liquid. Remove bones and skin.

- Stir in egg and cracker crumbs with salmon in bowl.

- In separate bowl, combine baking powder to ¼ cup salmon liquid. (Mixture will foam.) After foaming, add to salmon mixture.

- Drop teaspoonfuls of mixture on hot skillet. Brown lightly on both sides. Serve hot. Serves 4 to 6.

Baked Halibut Supreme

2 (1 inch thick) halibut steaks
1 (8 ounce) carton sour cream
½ cup grated parmesan cheese
¾ teaspoon dill weed

- Preheat oven to 325°.

- Place halibut in sprayed 9 x 13-inch baking dish.

- Combine sour cream, parmesan cheese and dill weed. Spoon over halibut. Cover and bake at for about 20 minutes.

- Uncover and bake for additional 10 minutes or until fish flakes easily with fork. Serves 6 to 8.

Curried Red Snapper

1½ pounds fresh red snapper
1 teaspoon curry powder
¼ cup milk

- Preheat oven to 350°.

- Place snapper in sprayed 9 x 13-inch baking pan.

- Combine curry powder and milk and mix well. Spoon over snapper.

- Bake for 25 minutes or until fish flakes easily with fork. Serves 4.

Tip: You can find a package of frozen chopped bell peppers, onions and celery in the frozen foods section of your local supermarket. You can cook 1 cup of it for a few minutes in a little butter in the baking dish, add the snapper on top and follow the recipe above. The snapper is great just as it is, but some people like the hint of vegetables in the sauce. The real tip here is that you don't have to buy vegetables and chop them. You can find them already chopped.

Cheesy Tuna Bake

1 (8 ounce) package crescent rolls, divided
1 (6 ounce) can solid white tuna in water, drained, flaked
1 (15 ounce) can cut asparagus, drained
1 cup shredded cheddar cheese

- Preheat oven to 375°.

- Form 7-inch square using 4 crescent rolls. Pinch edges together to seal. Place in sprayed 8-inch square baking pan.

- Layer tuna, asparagus and cheese on top.

- Form remaining 4 crescent rolls into 1 square. Place on top of cheese.

- Bake for about 20 minutes or until top is golden brown and cheese bubbles. Serves 6.

Simple Shrimp Newburg

1 (10 ounce) can cream of shrimp soup
1 teaspoon seafood seasoning
1 (1 pound) package frozen cooked salad shrimp, thawed
White rice, cooked

- Combine soup, ¼ cup water and seafood seasoning in saucepan and bring to a boil.

- Reduce heat and stir in shrimp. Heat thoroughly. Serve over white rice. Serves 4.

THE MOST IMPORTANT THING TO REMEMBER ABOUT COOKING FISH IS NOT TO OVERCOOK IT. THE INTERNAL TEMPERATURE SHOULD BE ABOUT 145° AND THE FLESH SHOULD BE OPAQUE. DON'T LET FISH DRY OUT.

Broiled Lemon-Garlic Shrimp

1 pound shrimp, peeled, veined
1 teaspoon garlic salt

2 tablespoons lemon juice
2 tablespoons butter

- Place shrimp in shallow baking pan. Sprinkle with garlic salt and lemon juice and dot with butter.
- Broil on 1 side for 3 minutes. Turn and broil for additional 3 minutes. Serves 4.

Tip: If shrimp are large, split them down middle and spread them out like a butterfly before seasoning.

Skillet Shrimp Magic

2 teaspoons olive oil
2 pounds shrimp, peeled, veined
2/3 cup herb-garlic marinade with lemon juice

1/4 cup finely chopped green onions with tops

- Heat oil in large non-stick skillet. Add shrimp and marinade.
- Cook, stirring often, until shrimp turn pink. Stir in green onions. Serves 4 to 6.

Tip: This is a wonderful shrimp dish. Serve as is or over rice or your favorite pasta.

Easy Boiled Shrimp

3 pounds fresh shrimp
2 teaspoons seafood seasoning

½ cup vinegar
1 teaspoon salt

- Remove heads from shrimp.

- Place shrimp, salt, seasoning and vinegar in large saucepan. Cover shrimp with water and bring to a boil.

- Reduce heat and boil for 10 minutes. Remove from heat, drain and refrigerate. Serves 8.

Crusted Baked Oysters

1 cup oysters, drained, rinsed
2 cups cracker crumbs

¼ cup (½ stick) butter, melted
½ cup milk

- Preheat oven to 350°.

- Make alternate layers of oysters, cracker crumbs and butter in sprayed 8-inch square baking dish.

- Warm milk in saucepan and pour over layers. Bake for about 15 to 20 minutes. Serves 4.

Vegetables and Side Dishes

Easy Lemon Broccoli

1 (16 ounce) frozen package of broccoli florets
¼ cup (½ stick) butter

1 tablespoon lemon juice
½ teaspoon salt

- Cook broccoli according to package directions and drain.

- Melt butter in saucepan and stir in lemon juice and salt.

- Pour over broccoli and toss to coat. Serves 4.

Cheddar-Broccoli Bake

1 (10 ounce) can cheddar cheese soup
½ cup milk
1 (16 ounce) bag frozen broccoli

florets, cooked
1 (3 ounce) can french-fried onions

- Preheat oven to 350°.

- Mix soup, milk and broccoli in 2-quart baking dish. Bake for 25 minutes.

- Stir and sprinkle fried onions over broccoli mixture. Bake for additional 5 minutes or until onions are golden. Serves 6.

Creamy Vegetable Casserole

1 (16 ounce) package frozen
   broccoli, carrots and
   cauliflower
1 (10 ounce) can cream of
   mushroom soup

1 (8 ounce) carton garden-
   vegetable cream cheese
1 cup seasoned croutons

- Preheat oven to 350°.

- Cook vegetables according to package directions, drain and place in large bowl.

- Combine soup and cream cheese in saucepan and heat just enough to mix easily.

- Pour into vegetable mixture and mix well. Pour into 2-quart baking dish.

- Sprinkle with croutons. Bake for 25 minutes or until bubbly. Serves 6 to 8.

Creamy Asparagus Bake

2 (15 ounce) cans cut asparagus
   spears with liquid
3 eggs, hard-boiled, chopped

½ cup chopped pecans
1 (10 ounce) can cream of celery
   soup

- Preheat oven to 350°.

- Arrange asparagus spears in sprayed 2-quart baking dish. Top with eggs and pecans.

- Heat asparagus soup and add liquid from asparagus spears.

- Spoon over eggs and pecans. Cover and bake for 25 minutes. Serves 8.

Corn Pudding ～～～～～～～～～～～

*1 (8 ounce) package corn muffin
    mix
1 (15 ounce) can cream-style corn*

*½ cup sour cream
3 eggs, slightly beaten*

- Preheat oven to 350°.

- Combine all ingredients in bowl and pour into sprayed 2-quart
  baking dish.

- Bake for about 35 minutes. Serves 6.

Wild West Corn ～～～～～～～～～

*2 (15 ounce) cans whole kernel
    corn, drained
1 (10 ounce) can diced tomatoes
    and green chilies, drained*

*1 (8 ounce) package shredded
    Monterey Jack cheese
1 cup cheese cracker crumbs*

- Preheat oven to 350°.

- Combine corn, tomatoes and green chilies, and cheese in large
  bowl and mix well.

- Pour into sprayed 2½-quart baking dish.

- Sprinkle cracker crumbs over casserole. Bake for 25 minutes.
  Serves 4 to 6.

Easy Lemon Broccoli ～～～～～～～～

*1 (16 ounce) frozen package of
    broccoli florets
¼ cup (½ stick) butter*

*1 tablespoon lemon juice
½ teaspoon salt*

- Cook broccoli according to package directions and drain.

- Melt butter in saucepan and stir in lemon juice and salt.

- Pour over broccoli and toss to coat. Serves 4.

Eggplant Casserole

1 large eggplant
1 cup cracker crumbs
1 cup shredded cheddar cheese,
  divided

1 (10 ounce) can diced tomatoes
  and green chilies

- Preheat oven to 350°.

- Peel and slice eggplant.

- Place eggplant in saucepan and cover with water. Cook for
  10 minutes or until tender. Drain well on paper towels.

- Mash eggplant. Stir in cracker crumbs, ¾ cup cheese, and tomatoes
  and green chilies and mix well.

- Spoon eggplant mixture in sprayed 1-quart baking dish. Sprinkle
  with remaining cheese. Bake for 30 minutes. Serves 8.

Italian Green Beans

1 (16 ounce) package frozen
  Italian green beans
3 green onions with tops, chopped

2 tablespoons butter
1 teaspoon Italian seasoning

- Mix all ingredients plus ¼ cup water in 2-quart saucepan.

- Cook on medium-high heat for about 10 minutes or until beans are
  tender. Serves 6.

Seasoned Green Beans

4 slices bacon, chopped
1 medium onion, chopped
2 (15 ounce) cans green beans,

drained
1 teaspoon sugar

- Saute bacon and onion in skillet and drain.

- Add green beans and sugar and heat thoroughly. Serves 8.

Favorite Spinach Casserole ~~~~~~

2 (10 ounce) packages frozen
  chopped spinach, thawed, well
  drained*
1 (1 ounce) packet onion soup mix

1 (8 ounce) carton sour cream
2/3 cup shredded Monterey Jack
  cheese

- Preheat oven to 350°.

- Combine spinach, onion soup mix and sour cream. Pour into sprayed 2-quart baking dish. Bake for 20 minutes.

- Take out of oven, sprinkle cheese over top and place casserole back in oven for 5 minutes. Serves 8.

*Tip: Squeeze spinach between paper towels
   to completely remove excess moisture.

Posh Squash ~~~~~~~~~~~~~

8 medium yellow squash, sliced
½ green bell pepper, seeded,
  chopped
1 small onion, chopped

1 (8 ounce) package shredded
  Mexican processed cheese

- Preheat oven to 350°.

- Combine squash, bell pepper and onion in large saucepan and just barely cover with water.

- Cook just until tender for about 10 to 15 minutes.

- Drain and add cheese. Stir until cheese melts and pour into sprayed 2-quart baking dish.

- Bake for 15 minutes. Serves 6 to 8.

Southern-Fried Zucchini

3 large zucchini, grated
5 eggs

⅓ (12 ounce) box round buttery
    crackers, crushed
Oil

- Combine zucchini, eggs and cracker crumbs in bowl and mix well.
  Add cheese.

- Drop spoonfuls of mixture into skillet with a little oil. Fry for about
  15 minutes and brown on each side. Serves 8.

*Tip: For an extra treat, add 1 cup grated parmesan
cheese to mixture before browning.*

Herbed Spinach

2 (16 ounce) packages frozen
    chopped spinach
1 (8 ounce) package cream
    cheese, softened

¼ cup (½ stick) butter, melted,
    divided
1 (6 ounce) package herbed-
    seasoned stuffing

- Preheat oven to 350°.

- Cook spinach according to package directions. Squeeze spinach
  between paper towels to completely remove excess moisture.

- Add cream cheese and half butter.

- Pour into sprayed baking dish. Spread herb stuffing on top and
  drizzle with remaining butter.

- Bake for 25 minutes. Serves 8.

Loaded Baked Potatoes

6 medium potatoes
1 (1 pound) package hot sausage
1 (16 ounce) package cubed
   processed American cheese

1 (10 ounce) can diced tomatoes
   and green chilies, drained

- Preheat oven to 375°.

- Wrap potatoes in foil and bake for 1 hour or until done.

- Brown sausage in skillet and drain.

- Add cheese to sausage and heat until cheese melts. Add tomatoes
  and green chilies. Serve sausage-cheese mixture over baked
  potatoes. Serves 6.

Easy Oven-Roasted Potatoes

2 pounds new (red) potatoes with
   peels
1 (1 ounce) packet onion soup mix

$^{1}/_{3}$ cup olive oil
½ teaspoon pepper

- Preheat oven to 425°.

- Wash potatoes and cut into bite-size pieces. Add all ingredients in
  large resealable bag. Shake until potatoes coat evenly.

- Empty coated potatoes into sprayed 9 x 13-inch baking pan.

- Bake, stirring twice, for 40 minutes or until golden brown. Serves 8.

Sweet Potato Casserole ~~~~~~~~

1 (28 ounce) can sweet potatoes,
    drained
½ cup chopped pecans

1½ cups packed light brown
    sugar
½ cup (1 stick) butter, melted

- Preheat oven to 350°.

- Slice sweet potatoes into 2-quart baking dish. Sprinkle pecans over sweet potatoes.

- Make syrup of brown sugar and butter with just enough water to make it thin enough to pour in saucepan. Bring to a boil and pour syrup over sweet potatoes.

- Bake for 30 minutes or until potatoes brown. Serves 4 to 6.

Southern-Fried Zucchini ~~~~~~~~

3 large zucchini, grated
5 eggs

⅓ (12 ounce) box round buttery
    crackers, crushed
Oil

- Combine zucchini, eggs and cracker crumbs in bowl and mix well. Add cheese.

- Drop spoonfuls of mixture into skillet with a little oil. Fry for about 15 minutes and brown on each side. Serves 8.

*Tip: For an extra treat, add 1 cup grated parmesan cheese
    to mixture before browning.*

Seasoned Brown Rice

1 cup rice
1 (10 ounce) can French onion
  soup

1 (10 ounce) can beef broth
3 tablespoons butter, melted

- Preheat oven to 350°.

- Place rice in sprayed 2-quart baking dish. Combine soup, broth and butter in bowl. Pour over rice.

- Cover and bake for 45 minutes. Serves 4 to 6.

Creamy Pasta Side

1 (8 ounce) jar roasted red
  peppers, drained
1 (14 ounce) can chicken broth

1 (3 ounce) package cream cheese
1 (8 ounce) package favorite
  pasta, cooked

- Combine red peppers and broth in blender and mix well. Pour into saucepan and heat to boiling.

- Turn heat down and whisk in cream cheese, mixing until cream cheese melts. Serve over your favorite pasta. Serves 6.

Special Macaroni and Cheese

1 (8 ounce) package small
  macaroni shells
1 (15 ounce) can stewed tomatoes

1 (8 ounce) package cubed
  processed American cheese
3 tablespoons butter, melted

- Preheat oven to 350°.

- Cook shells according to package directions in saucepan and drain.

- Combine shells, tomatoes, cheese cubes and butter in large bowl.

- Pour into sprayed 2-quart baking dish. Cover and bake for 35 minutes. Serves 6 to 8.

Desserts

Lemon Pie Treat

1 (3 ounce) package lemon pie
    filling mix
⅓ cup sugar

1 egg, slightly beaten
½ (8 ounce) carton whipped
    topping

- Mix pie filling, sugar and egg with ¼ cup water in saucepan until smooth. Slowly add another 1¾ cups water.

- Cook, stirring constantly, over medium heat until mixture comes to a full boil. Remove from heat and cool to room temperature.

- Fold in whipped topping and spoon into individual dessert dishes. Serves 6.

Divine Strawberries

This is wonderful served over pound cake or just served in sherbet glasses.

1 quart fresh strawberries, cored
1 (20 ounce) can pineapple
    chunks, well drained

2 bananas, sliced
2 (16 ounce) carton strawberry
    glaze

- Cut strawberries in half (or in quarters if strawberries are very large).

- Combine strawberries, pineapple chunks and bananas in bowl.

- Fold in strawberry glaze and refrigerate. Serves 6 to 8.

Easy Boiled Custard

1 (14 ounce) can sweetened
    condensed milk
1 quart milk

4 eggs
½ teaspoon vanilla

- Combine sweetened condensed milk and milk and heat in double boiler.

- Beat eggs well in bowl. Slowly pour milk, a little at a time, over eggs, stirring constantly.

- Gradually add eggs to milk and cook on low for 5 to 10 minutes, stirring constantly, until mixture thickens.

- Stir in vanilla and refrigerate. Serves 8.

Tip: This may be served in custard cups or stemmed glasses.

Fudgy Ice Cream Dessert

19 ice cream sandwiches
1 (12 ounce) carton whipped
    topping, thawed

1 (12 ounce) jar hot fudge ice
    cream topping
1 cup salted peanuts, divided

- Cut 1 ice cream sandwich in half. Place 1 whole and one-half sandwich along short side of 9 x 13-inch pan. Arrange 8 sandwiches in opposite direction in pan.

- Spread with half whipped topping. Spoon teaspoonfuls of fudge topping onto whipped topping. Sprinkle with ½ cup peanuts.

- Repeat layers with remaining ice cream sandwiches, whipped topping and peanuts (pan will be full). Cover and freeze. Serves 12.

Tip: To serve, take out of freezer 20 minutes before serving.

Almond-Capped Peach Sundaes

1 (1 pint) carton vanilla ice cream
¾ cup peach preserves, warmed

¼ cup chopped almonds, toasted
¼ cup flaked coconut

- Divide ice cream into 4 sherbet dishes. Top with preserves.
- Sprinkle with almonds and coconut. Serves 4.

Peanut Butter Sundae

1 cup light corn syrup
1 cup crunchy peanut butter

¼ cup milk
Ice cream or pound cake

- Stir corn syrup, peanut butter and milk in bowl until they blend well.
- Serve over ice cream or pound cake. Store in refrigerator. Serves 4.

Basic Pound Cake

1½ cups (3 sticks) butter, softened
3 cups sugar

8 eggs
3 cups sifted flour

- Preheat oven to 300°.
- Cream butter and sugar in bowl and mix well.
- Add eggs one at a time and beat well after each addition. Add flour in small amounts at a time.
- Pour into sprayed, floured 10-inch bundt pan and bake for 1 hour 30 minutes. Do not open oven door during baking. Serves 12.

Chocolate Pudding Cake

1 (18 ounce) box milk chocolate cake mix	1/3 cup canola oil
1¼ cups milk	3 eggs

- Preheat oven to 350°.
- Combine all ingredients in bowl and beat well.
- Pour into sprayed, floured 9 x 13-inch baking pan.
- Bake for 35 minutes or when toothpick inserted in center comes out clean.

Chocolate Pudding Cake Frosting:

This is a very good, quick frosting on any cake.

1 (14 ounce) can sweetened condensed milk	1 (8 ounce) carton whipped topping, thawed
¾ (16 ounce) can chocolate syrup	1/3 cup chopped pecans

- Mix sweetened condensed milk and chocolate syrup in small bowl.
- Pour over cake and let soak into cake. Refrigerate for several hours.
- Spread whipped topping over top of cake and sprinkle pecans on top. Refrigerate. Serves 12.

Emergency Cheesecake

1 (8 ounce) package cream cheese, softened	½ cup lemon juice
1 (14 ounce) can sweetened condensed milk	1 (6 ounce) ready graham cracker piecrust

- Beat all ingredients in bowl. Pour into piecrust and refrigerate.

Serves 8.

Quick Apple Cake

1 (18 ounce) box spiced cake mix   2 eggs
1 (20 ounce) can apple pie filling $^{1}/_{3}$ cup chopped walnuts

- Preheat oven to 350°.

- Combine all ingredients in bowl and mix very thoroughly with spoon. Make sure all lumps from cake mix break up.

- Pour into sprayed, floured bundt pan. Bake for 50 minutes or when toothpick inserted in center comes out clean. Serves 10 to 12.

Tip: You may substitute any other pie filling for this cake.

Easy Pineapple Cake

2 cups sugar   1 (20 ounce) can crushed
2 cups flour   pineapple with liquid
                                     1 teaspoon baking soda

- Preheat oven to 350°.

- Combine all ingredients in bowl and mix with spoon.

- Pour into sprayed, floured 9 x 13-inch baking pan. Bake for 30 to 35 minutes.

Easy Pineapple Cake Topping:

1 (8 ounce) package cream   1 cup powdered sugar
   cheese, softened   1 cup chopped pecans
½ cup (1 stick) butter, melted

- Beat cream cheese, butter and powdered sugar in bowl

- Add chopped pecans and spoon over hot cake. Serves 12.

Pound Cake Deluxe

1 (10 inch) round bakery pound
  cake
1 (20 ounce) can crushed
  pineapple
  with liquid

1 (5 ounce) package coconut
  instant pudding mix
1 (8 ounce) carton whipped
  topping

- Slice cake horizontally to make 3 layers. Mix pineapple, pudding
  and whipped topping in bowl and blend well.

- Spread on each layer and top of cake. Refrigerate. Serves 12.

Easy Pumpkin Pie

2 eggs
1 (30 ounce) can pumpkin pie mix

1 (5 ounce) can evaporated milk
1 (9 inch) deep-dish piecrust

- Preheat oven to 400°.

- Beat eggs lightly in large bowl. Stir in pumpkin pie mix and
  evaporated milk. Pour mixture into piecrust.

- Cut 2-inch strips of foil and cover crust edges to prevent excessive
  browning.

- Bake for 15 minutes. Reduce temperature to 325° and bake for
  additional 40 minutes or until knife inserted in center comes out
  clean. Cool. Serves 8.

Three-Step Blueberry Cobbler

2 (20 ounce) cans blueberry pie
    filling
1 (18 ounce) box white cake mix

1 egg
½ cup (1 stick) butter, softened

- Preheat oven to 350°.

- Spread pie filling in sprayed 9 x 13-inch baking dish.

- Combine cake mix, egg and butter in bowl and blend well. Mixture will be stiff. Spoon filling over top.

- Bake for 45 minutes or until golden brown. Serves 12 to 14.

Butter Cookie Special

1 (18 ounce) box butter cake mix
1 (3.4 ounce) package butterscotch
    instant pudding mix

1 cup canola oil
1 egg, beaten

- Preheat oven to 350°.

- Combine cake mix, pudding mix, oil and egg in bowl and mix with spoon. Beat thoroughly.

- Drop teaspoonfuls of dough onto cookie sheet about 2 inches apart.

- Bake for about 8 minutes. Do not overcook. Yields 3 dozen.

Oreo Cake

1 (18 ounce) box white cake mix
⅓ cup canola oil
4 egg whites

2¼ cups coarsely chopped Oreo cookies

- Preheat oven to 350°.

- Combine cake mix, oil, 1¼ cups water and egg whites in bowl. Blend on low speed until moist. Beat for 2 minutes at high speed.

- Gently fold in 1¼ cups coarsely chopped cookies. Pour batter into 2 sprayed, floured 8-inch round cake pans.

- Bake for 25 to 30 minutes or until toothpick inserted in center comes out clean.

- Cool for 15 minutes and remove from pan. Cool completely and frost.

Oreo Cake Frosting

4¼ cups powdered sugar
1 cup (2 sticks) butter, softened

1 cup shortening (not butter-flavored)
1 teaspoon almond flavoring

- Combine all ingredients in bowl and beat until creamy.

- Frost first layer of cake and place second layer on top and frost top and sides.

- Sprinkle with remaining crushed Oreo cookies on top.
Serves 12.